A Long Time to Be Gone

Books by Michael McFee

Poetry

Plain Air
Vanishing Acts
Sad Girl Sitting on a Running Board
To See
Colander
Earthly
Shinemaster
That Was Oasis
We Were Once Here

Poetry chapbooks

The Smallest Talk
Never Closer

Prose

The Napkin Manuscripts: Selected Essays and an Interview
Appointed Rounds: Essays

As editor

*The Language They Speak Is Things to Eat: Poems by 15 Contemporary
    North Carolina Poets*
*This Is Where We Live: Short Stories by 25 Contemporary North
    Carolina Writers*
The Spectator Reader

A Long Time to Be Gone

Michael McFee

Carnegie Mellon University Press
Pittsburgh 2022

Acknowledgments

Thanks to the editors of these magazines, for publishing first versions of these poems:

Appalachian Journal: "The Valley of the Shadow," "When," "Festival," "Mutch";
Birmingham Poetry Review: "A Rusty"; *Cincinnati Review*: "Banister Slide"; *Four Way Review*: "Lethe," "Hnnnh"; *Hudson Review*: "Brother Ass," "Palms," "Parking Garage," "The word," "Manual Typewriter," "'Richard Burton,'" "'In a Sentimental Mood'"; *ONE*: "Smoking"; *River Styx*: "George Washington"; *Southern Poetry Review*: "Dog, Drinking"; *Southern Review*: "Virgule," "Skull Orchard," "Autographs" ; *Still: The Journal*: "A Grudge"; *Stone Canoe*: "The Cloud"; *Tar River Poetry*: "The Dwindles," "Nearly," "Table Muscle," "Teeninecy," "Wee"

Thanks to the editors of these anthologies, for publishing first versions of these poems:

Chapters & Verses: Stories and Poems from the Creative Writing Program at Carolina, edited by Daniel Wallace (Department of English and Comparative Literature, UNC-Chapel Hill, 2021): "Before," "STAY HOME"; *A Literary Field Guide to Southern Appalachia*, edited by Rose McLarney and Laura-Gray Street (University of Georgia Press, 2019): "Please"; *The Store of Joys: Writers Celebrate the North Carolina Museum of Art's Fiftieth Anniversary*, edited by Huston Paschal (Blair, 1997): "The Gospel According to Minnie Evans"; *You Are the River: Literature Inspired by the North Carolina Museum of Art*, edited by Helena Federer (NCMA, 2021): "Portrait of the Poet as Saint Jerome"

"Virgule" was reprinted by the Academy of American Poets at their poets.org website.

Thanks to the U. S. Department of Agriculture Pomological Water Collection, Rare and Special Collections, National Agricultural Library, Beltsville, Maryland, for the cover image of a McAfee's Nonsuch apple from Pittstown, Pennsylvania, painted by Mary Daisy Arnold in 1912.

Thanks also to the Department of English and Comparative Literature, UNC-Chapel Hill, for a Research and Study Assignment, which made it possible for me to complete this book.

And thanks, again and always, to Michael Chitwood, for his notes on every poem and essay I write.

Book design by Martina Rethman

Library of Congress Control Number 2022942280
ISBN 978-0-88748-686-9
Copyright © 2022 by Michael McFee
All rights reserved
Printed and bound in the United States of America

10 9 8 7 6 5 4 3 2 1

for Gerald Costanzo, Jonathan Greene,
and all my book publishers through the years

Contents

1.

2. Coronavirus Variations

3.

4.

1.

Brother Ass

That's what Saint Francis called his body,
an obstinate donkey
he'd beat or walk through a briar patch
or heave headfirst into a snowbank, naked—
a dumb beast, loud and filthy,
whose frank appetites were an offense to God.

I mortified my body for half a century
by simply ignoring it,
taking a strong back and endurance for granted,
feeding and watering and grooming fitfully,
making it carry way too much
for far too long. That's what pack animals do.

Brother Ass is sturdy, sure-footed, patient.
He knows when to kick.
Now when I laugh, it's his long-eared big head
that brays, baring crooked yellow teeth,
teaching me how to be humble—
my fellow friar, my twin, my poor balky burro.

Lethe

"Sliding down the banks of the River Lethe as I am presently,"
my friend begins his paper letter: senior citizen's gallows humor.

I smile but wonder: is it a steep drop into that mythical water,

past rocks and roots and holes where slick Hades critters dwell,
or a gradual slippery slope across flood-combed weeds and clay

where you could grab something and dig in your heels and stop?

Is that underworld river cold or mild, its current slow or swift?
If you fall in, can your feet gain purchase and clamber out?

Even if your mouth stays shut and you manage not to swallow,

does forgetfulness nevertheless soak bare skin and wash away
the memory of everything you said and did and were on earth

before emerging downstream in your next life, a tabula rasa?

Maybe he was saying *I feel lethargic these days*, not *I'm dying.*
Or maybe he was sending a signal that he already finds himself

in oblivion's headwaters, dog-paddling, struggling to remember

how to keep his brain above the flow as he's being swept away,
no ferryboat emerging from darkness and fog to rescue him.

Hnnnh

A little grunt escapes the old man's mouth

every time he stands up, or sits, or has to shift,
a strained audible exhale signaling effort,

ghost of a come-groan, a going-away syllable,

an involuntary exasperating geezer noise
saying *I'm weary and I hurt* without saying it,

as if the air's being squeezed out of his body

bit by bit until the day he can't move at all—
wait: that's my grunting now. My low *hnnnh*.

The Dwindles

"If she lives two more years, she probably won't have any hair at all,"
said my neighbor about his balding Maltese

wheezing at my feet, epidermis mottled and tail naked, an ongoing
humiliation of shedding she couldn't see,

being mostly blind as well: "I guess she's got the dwindles," he laughed,
though I didn't, knowing she was pretty much

my age in dog years, thinking how my body's hair was doing its own
disappearing act. I scratched her flushed skin;

she grumbled, bare stub wagging. What tall creature may kneel to offer
a hand as I continue to diminish, lifting me up

to carry indoors when it's dark, repeating *good boy* into my bad ear?

Banister Slide

It's been way too long
since I sat on a handrail
in an open stairwell
and let gravity help me
descend to the next level,
arms and legs extended
for precarious balance
as I surf a frozen wave,
pants buffing the banister
while I glide over the steps
my feet don't have to take
to get down to the bottom
where I leap off, a kid
grinning at his shortcut,
his speed, his nonchalant
ability to make his body
do exactly what he wants:
execute this flying fall
then stick the landing
and walk off like nothing
unlikely just happened.

Palms

Hands' pale soles,
digits' footing,

tender flip side
of knock and punch,

they blush if forced
to clap, so public,

and timidly sweat
when clasped, shaken.

Palms are your pages
in fortune's book:

strangers can be paid
to read their lines.

Waved, the body's
hail or farewell;

its flag of surrender
if emptied, raised.

Nearly

Approaching the bridge over the busy boulevard,
I see a man running from his car, hastily parked,

toward a crying teenage girl in a tank top and skirt

straddling the rail, leaning toward afternoon traffic
slowing beneath her as I myself am slowing down

but not stopping, not wanting to provoke anything,

passing by then watching in my rearview mirror
as the man edges closer, closer, hands up, talking:

I call 9-1-1 and provide the few details gathered

in a few seconds a few blocks away from my house,
not pulling off to gape at the drama developing

between those two, negotiating in such perilous air,

and the dispatched cops who should arrive soon,
though when I drive back to the rusted bridge

in ten tense minutes, fearing the worst, it's empty,

not a soul in sight, nobody standing on its deck
or unbalanced on its metal bars or lying below it,

no sign of anything dire having nearly happened.

Parking Garage

1.

This morning, after rush hour, the only spaces left
were on the roofless top of the hospital parking garage.

My car's the last one up here now, well past sunset,
the city glowing below, scattered stars feebly shining,
the dark graphs of the mountains' rise and fall
an unreadable record surrounding us at the horizon.

I get in, lower the windows, and begin my descent.

2.

This structure's like a high-rise office building
abandoned before it was finished, no interior walls,
no windows installed to keep the weather outside,

just stacks of concrete plateaus and tight-turn spirals
creaking under my radials as I maintain a slow roll
forward and downward, worrying about my father
who's completing a month in cardiac intensive care.

3.

I don't know it, but tonight will be his last on earth,
with strangers on the seventh floor of St. Joseph's,
in the hometown he only left for World War II.
For sixty years, dad drove its up-and-down streets.

He hated paying for parking, at the curb or in a lot:
may his afterlife be nothing like this deck, my father
not forced to circle and circle, looking for a spot.

4.

The unclaimed vehicles are asleep, quiet and dark.

I'm the only living being navigating these strata,
fumbling for the time-stamped ticket I jammed
into my jacket pocket with all the medical papers
I signed, dated, then hid as quickly as possible.

Ghosts of exhaust and rubber, of piss and cigarettes
haunt the tiered cave as I sink, hauling my echo.

5.

I take a final left onto Ground Level, gently coasting
toward the attendant's booth, wallet waiting on the seat.

But that glass hut is empty, its take-out window shut,
no dingy angel there to guard the entrance and exit,
the gate arm raised like a salute as I drive into the night

dizzied by hospital halls and my circuit of this garage,
leaving its poorly-lit emptiness looming behind me.

Before

My mom would let me pull the golden strip
around the top of her pack of Philip Morris,
carefully removing the crackling transparent flap
of cellophane snugly sealing the cigarettes

whose tips I'd press against my nose, eyes closed,
inhaling the unlit king-size class A
unfiltered Commanders she'd enjoy all day,
reducing twenty tobacco tubes to ash:

for a few crinkling seconds I smelled nothing
but sweetness, ripened leaves, a rich aroma
like the air in her country brother's brightleaf barn,
filling my flue-cured blissed-out head before

the match, the strike, the glow, the sucked-in cheeks,
the smoke blown in my face as I smiled, choked.

In Memory of My Niece

A year to the day after you died, a brown thrasher
perches outside the last window you looked out of

then sings, sings, his long tail deftly tilting earthward

and forward under the clenched gardenia branch,
that motion counterbalancing the force of his mimicry

with every loud phrase he broadcasts, simple physics

of a songbird's body in a bush: but my eyes can't
not imagine a ghost keeps pressing that feathery lever

just to hear the outburst of paired notes again, again.

Please

take what's left of me, desiccated stormcloud
    of bonegrit inside a weighty bag inside a box,
up the high way to Pisgah or Craggy Gardens
    in June, when acres of Catawba rhododendron
are blooming, as they were on our honeymoon,
    their purple panoply stretched across the ridges
so dazzling our camera's film was overwhelmed,
    everything belilaced—sky, mountain, valley, us.
Carry me upslope deep into those dense thickets
    locals once called hells, near-impassable tangles
of trunks and branches and dark leathery leaves,
    lofty mazes that lost pilgrims might not escape
if not for this narrow path first blazed by bears,
    more like a stray slick creek bed than a trail.
Linger a while in that dim sanctuary, surrounded
    by coolness, inhaling the bracing peaty tang
and the faint perfume of the rose-tree blossoms
    far overhead being appreciated all afternoon
by honeybees bumbling and humming their way
    into cupped flowers, the sweetest angelic buzz.
Then kneel (please) and leave what's left of me
    in that shade, safe from sun and wind and snow,
spreading my ashes at the foot of a vast shrub
    whose late spring crown is invisible as its roots
though you know it's there, a roof of brief glory
    high over me, hidden in that evergreen heaven.

2.

Coronavirus Variations

*Spring 2020, first months of the pandemic,
Durham, NC*

Names

COVID-19 sounds like sci-fi,
a computer-named deep-space death star
threatening apocalyptic doom
to the rest of the unsuspecting universe.

But *coronavirus* is mellifluous,
its opening syllables a luminous crown
around risen sun or moon,
around the heads of happy human beings.

And *novel coronavirus* sounds
so fresh, a fat book to read on the beach
in Mexico, drinking cerveza,
enjoying another slow cigar before sunset.

Its names hinge on labiodental *v*,
that bite the start of *virus*, Latin for poison
or oozing slime or nasty odor,
infectious agent shutting down the system.

The word

pandemic is framed by the word *panic*,
we the people fearfully emptying shelves

of toilet paper, water, antimicrobials, masks,
guns, stuff we can buy and hold and hoard

that might help us survive this purgatory,
praying our earthly paradise won't be lost

and we're not headed to *Pandemonium*,
a place invented by a blind poet yet real,

all the demons swarming that dark capital,
its air brusht with the hiss of rustling wings.

An Image

The CDC's electron microscope photograph
looks like a satellite or a cartoon planet
orbiting deep inside infected cells,
red protein spikes surrounding gray virion sphere,
high-resolution ultrastructual morphology.

It's not an artist's rendering, as in the past,
a sketch or watercolor made in the lab,
an image for what non-scientists can't imagine,

and yet it is, the black and white likeness real
but then highlighted by the researchers
to draw attention to its most dramatic parts:
"Generally," said a spokesman, "we color viruses
sort of these hot colors, such as red."

It's no longer a mystery if citizens can see it,
even if what they see is a doctored image
done with the best intentions, for the greater good.

The Valley of the Shadow

I see Psalm 23:4 on the closed church's sign—
though I walk through the valley of the shadow
of death, I will fear no evil, for thou art with me—

and remember reciting it together before class,
not during Sunday School but in second grade
at Valley Springs Elementary, such dutiful kids,

shadowed by the surrounding blue ridges,
all of us standing to utter David's holy words
after pledging our allegiance to the corner flag,

small palms over small hearts, puzzled perhaps
by *thy rod and thy staff, they comfort me*, yea,
but mumbling our way in unison to the end,

to the verse one of my buddies misheard as
Surely good Mrs. Murphy shall follow me
all the days of my life, a creepy widow lady

not unlike the teacher leading our recitations:
The Lord is my shepherd, I shall not want
she said, and believed, though that's hard to do

this spring when churches as well as schools
are locked and silent and still, as we continue
to dwell apart, in isolated houses, not the Lord's,

for what feels like it might turn into *forever*.

No

No Opening Day this year, baseball's Easter,
the grass, basepaths, and mound reborn again.

No sweaty queues, no ushers checking tickets.
No mascots posing for pics with giddy kids.

No fans flooding the stadium, finding seats.
No sloppy vendors, passing down food or beer.

No national anthem mangled by a glee club.
No managers sharing lineup cards with umps.

No defense taking the field, loosening arms.
No batters practice-swinging, tugging at gloves.

No pitchers warming up with masked catchers.
No spitting onto leather, bare flesh, or turf.

No knees and shoulders touching in the dugout.
No bored relievers' horseplay in the bullpen.

No runs, no hits, no errors on the scoreboard.
No seventh-inning stretch, no *Take me out* . . .

No fireworks afterwards, bombs bursting in air:
just a forsaken tomb, closed on Opening Day.

Will These Hands Ne'er Be Clean?

I stand at my bathroom sink and keep soaping

these hands a dozen times a day, or more,
lathering up nails and cuticles and knuckles,

deep purlicues and anatomical snuffboxes,

fingerprints, joint creases, lines, ridges, pads,
the plump ball of the thumb, the knobby wrist,

scrubbing as if I could reach the underlying

muscles and tendons, the vessels, the skeleton,
obsessing over these complex extremities

less like two lovers appreciating each other,

their slippery ups and downs and ins and outs,
than detectives searching for forensic evidence:

I wash and wash and wash under too-hot water

while humming "Happy Birthday" at least twice
as the foamy murky runoff spirals, vanishing,

as I disinfect pestilent grip and swipe and touch,

Lady Macbething these hands, trying my best
to scrub out the spot I can't see and isn't there,

right?

Of Breath

Shortness of breath: one of the dreaded symptoms.
A chronic asthmatic, I know what that feels like.

One night, decades ago, I woke up gasping.
What heavy fog was choking my laboring chest?

On the front steps, I waited for first responders.
A fire truck roared up from the local station.

The young EMT held my oxygen mask in place.
He calmly exhaled clouds in February darkness.

It's less shortness of breath than shallowness.
There's scarce air left in the lungs' little sacs.

They tethered my dying father to a ventilator.
Could he hear its steady metallic hiss and click?

Sometimes we require a machine to help us breathe.
Sometimes we infect each other with our breath.

A Sign

I pull five letters out of the Scrabble bag:
a C, an O, a V, an I, a D.

I can't believe it. I show them to my wife,
I take a picture and text it to our son

to prove I haven't made the whole thing up
for the sake of a clever story I'll tell later.

We finish the game. All my tiles are cursed.
I lose to her by more than a hundred points.

I'll never forget the afternoon that word
spelled itself out across my wooden tray

one black capital letter after the other,
a sign the disease could surface anywhere.

Blowing Kisses

Smooching fingertips pressed to my mouth
as if to hush the farewell welling up

inside me, I gallantly sweep them away

with a backhand wave, a visual goodbye
brisk and modest as a peck on each cheek,

or a grander gesture if I'm feeling like

a hammy actor bidding *adieu* to family,
using both hands to gather dramatic busses

from my lips then toss them at the camera,

blowing kisses toward the disembodied faces
air-mailing their far-off X's back to me.

Unpunctuated

Our arms' unfilled parentheses open wide,
we air-hug yearned-for bodies long distance.

No more giddy high-five apostrophes.
No moist handshakes, those earnest ampersands.
No exclamation-point kisses on cheeks.

Ellipses measure the spaces still between us.
Nothing but periods for now. Full stop.

When

After passing through the Nashville restaurant

crowded with fans surprised to see her there
many years ago, Dolly whispered, *"They love it*

when I touch 'em," her warm manicured hand

laid on diners' shoulders briefly, a bright pat,
the fingers that wrote "I Will Always Love You"

delivering the Parton charge, a surge of energy

providing much-needed relief from loneliness,
the queen touching her subjects, and they her,

that mutual affection uplifting both parties

through nights and days and solitary times
when noisy public rooms like that are hushed,

when nobody is supposed to touch a stranger.

Festival

The harmonizer leaned into the microphone.
His lips were maybe an inch from the lead singer's.

They broadcast spittle with their word-shaped breath.
They shook sweat onto the stage and the front rows.

The pickers kept swapping instruments and tuning.
The dancers swung their partners, promenaded.

Our bodies resonated like well-played strings.
"Community spread" back then was a shared quilt.

All weekend, the festive faces glistened with song.
Got a short time to stay here. And a long time to be gone.

This Limbo

"We're all shut-ins at this time," someone wrote.
Confined to one's home, as from illness or infirmity.

But most of us aren't sick; we hope not to be,
convalescing preemptively in our sanatoriums.

Our only affliction: a bad case of cabin fever.
Prolonged stay in a remote or confined place.

Church elders would visit the shut-ins faithfully,
the fatherless and the widows in their affliction.

Nobody's visiting anybody anymore, at least
not inside houses, where wicked germs might be.

Has anyone ever actually climbed the walls?
Maybe some inmates, in prison's oblivion.

What to call this limbo where we're marooned?
Which afterlife do we wait on the border of?

Puzzles

Jungle birds, paintings, cathedrals, coral reefs—
exotic jigsaw likenesses that our fingers

can reassemble, fitting piece by piece by piece

at a slow-motion holiday-with-grandma pace,
a way to pass stranded blurred-together weeks

with tabletop challenges that can be figured out

while hiding from the virus, working puzzles
of any colorful images to take our minds off it,

cereal boxes, dogs, postcards, Golden Girls,

paperboard mosaics whose tabs and blanks
interlock till every shallow hole is filled

and we step back to see the finished likeness,

a flat picture punctured into a thousand clues
whose mystery we solve through trial and error

~~before breaking it apart back into the box~~

and continuing the search for another pastime
to help us puzzle our way to the other side.

The Other Side

We're all taking an overlong nap
though we weren't ready to go down
after lunch, fought it hard, hard,

then gave up, red-faced in our cribs,

sweaty, sleepy, caged, dreaming
about all the stuff we'll do once awake
and on the other side of the door,

moving freely in unsheltered air,

toddling at topmost speed toward
snacks, drinks, games, huggers, kissers,
eager to grasp everything we can.

STAY HOME

ordered the overhead dot-matrix traffic sign,
but my wife continued driving us to the home
of old friends for socially distanced happy hour

on their as-yet-unmown front lawn, a placid slope

of tall thick grass brimming with yellow flowers,
Carolina Buttercups nodding as we high-stepped
to a spot still warmed by late Saturday sun

then coordinated the spacing out of chairs

before opening separate bottles and pouring wine,
lifting glasses half-filled with chardonnay light,
crying *Cheers!,* sipping and laughing and chatting

about children, ball games, parties, books, travels

as we'd done so often back in unguarded days,
the four of us part of the yard's low green sky
and its tangled constellation of glowing blooms,

short-lived perennials, our radiance deepening.

3.

A Rusty

"He's sure cuttin' a rusty," she said, flatly,

my parents' elderly neighbor gazing down
at our furious toddler bawling and howling

and wallowing in Saturday afternoon weeds.

I'd never heard that term. It sounded right
for this child cutting up on her uncut yard,

the two *uhs* making their low vowel ruckus

in the mouth, the open-ended terminal *–ty*
providing crisp uplift after the tiniest hiss.

That night, in my childhood bed and bedroom,

breathing quietly beside my Piedmont wife,
our red-faced son finally spent and asleep,

I remembered growing up on this steep street

with a kid named Rusty, a furtive dirty boy
who ate dirt and even (on a dare) little rocks.

Was the neighbor recalling his gravelly yowls

as he rolled on the ground, clutching his belly?
She moved from a mountain cove to that suburb,

to be near her own come-to-town offspring.

Maybe she learned the phrase in Bloody Madison
among "the rustics," as one visitor called them,

uncouth clodhoppers pitchin' their hissy fits,

playin' the fool anytime the fancy took them,
drinkin' moonshine and firin' off their rifles.

"Unsophisticated boisterous misbehavior"—

ain't that what them ignorant hillbillies do?
Did I ever cut a rusty? I can't ask my parents:

they've been dead longer than I'd been alive

the time their rowdy grandson kept capering
at the feet of an implacable country woman.

Maybe I should rip one off if my doctor ever

delivers malignant news, falling to the tile floor,
"engaging in a grotesque, frolicsome action,"

loudly bewailing the fate I've just been dealt

but secretly enjoying that histrionic scene,
that chance to overreact again, that encore solo

outburst before I conclude the conniption

then rise to smooth out my clothes and smile,
bowing, shaking his cold hand, saying *So long.*

Virgule

Its perpendicular
tilted, falling forward,

this oblique stroke
between lines of verse

or fractions' numbers
or month/day/year

separates & connects
parts of some whole:

its diagonal can also
offer us alternatives

like his/her, either/or,
skinny twig partway

between limb & ground,
like me not quite vertical

or horizontal, a slash
leaning into stiff wind.

Manual Typewriter

What I almost miss

isn't keys smacking paper
I'd fed to the platen

but the hidden bell's *ding*

when my typing neared
the right-hand margin,

a cheerful sound meaning

another line done,
my left hand swiping

the carriage return lever

with only the slightest
pause in the rackety

outpouring of words

from a manual laborer
working a machine

with quick clever fingers

before the next chime
telling me I'd won,

another line done.

The Cloud

The annoyed IT guy explains yet again
why I need to be on or in or @ The Cloud,
so nothing important will ever be lost:

I guess it would be a good thing to sign up
for this heaven that won't cost me anything,
this digital eternal life insurance policy

he's witnessing about in such geeky detail,
I really should care more about saving copies
of what I've written on this fancy machine

but I'm not listening, I just wish he'd leave
so I can lay a blank sheet on my waiting desk
and draft a manuscript with a No. 2 pencil,

writing it slowly, letter by word by line,
seeing and hearing and touching the data
imagined by my cumulonimbus brain,

a shadow, a storm, maybe a lightning strike
charging the paper accessible only to me,
no passwords or anti-hacker encryption

needed for this suspension of fine particles
in the atmosphere above a planet's surface,
its flimsy brightness floating on my palm.

A Grudge

1.

She said, "You sure know how to hold a grudge."
Guilty as charged. That's one skill my parents

taught their children well, part of our heritage—

clutching a grudge tight, nursing a slight or insult
from kin or nearby clans who've dishonored us,

sipping its bitter spirits distilled out of sight

until the grievance explodes into a bloody feud
or simply turns inward, a private resentment

darkening the sore heart, a still-open wound

we can't seem to keep ourselves from poking,
secretly pleased to suffer that unhealed hurt.

2.

Grudge sounds like a kicked stray mutt growling,
its rough velar grumble ending in clenched teeth,

the aggrieved party grousing with every breath

while trudging forsaken ridges in stiff wind,
a grumpy descendent of gruesome highlanders

stirring the acrid sludge stuck inside his skull,

judging one by one by one the wrongs inflicted
on him, poor drudge, always the innocent party,

grunting as he stumbles on, plotting revenge.

3.

How satisfying, to convert such indignities
and irritation into something smooth, a pearl

nobody beholds inside your homely shell,

its worry stone a slowly growing treasure,
a roundness your fingers can't stop rubbing,

polishing the surface until it finally gleams

like a moon whose cold flat light reminds you
hate can be sweet and spitefulness endures.

It's Old Testamental: *Thou shalt bear a grudge*

against thine enemies forever, if they deserve it.
It may be all you have, when you have nothing.

Skull Orchard

Maybe *boneyard* wasn't bleak and specific enough

for that fatalist being recorded by an oral historian
deep in the North Georgia mountains, long ago,

maybe he was an apple farmer who'd had a bad year,
Black Limbertwig blossoms ruined by a late freeze:

his *skull orchard* does make us see the rows and rows

of those peculiar groves called cemeteries, gentle word
for such high density plantings of heirloom cultivars

precisely spaced with weatherproof names and dates,
the new heads' seeds joining a strata of bony bulbs

ready to light the darkness when the Rapture comes.

They wait six feet below, ancestral shadows cast deep.
Our brains move six feet above, heritage apples, ripe.

Table Muscle

was what he called it, with a fond proud pat,
that massive pod he'd fattened meal by meal
by meal at his mother's table, then his wife's,
then back to his mother's, its accretion of flesh
waxing against his shirt and unbuckled pants:
he ate and chuckled and wheezed but couldn't
stop fueling that potbelly, though its girth
unbalanced his body, tilting him forward
and shortening his stride as he walked away,
reluctantly, from breakfast, lunch, or dinner,
his appetite already imagining its next bite,
my uncle's profile a little rounder every day
as he carried that paunch in front of him
like a feedsack filled too full, about to split.

Teeninecy

simply felt smaller
than *tiny* or *teensy:*

it was long enough,
however, to sport
a framing e-rhyme
and the last largest
single-digit number
at its core, a syllable
to stress and stretch.

Never did that word
sound more mini
than when itty-bitty
Aunt Pinky would
push its triple-wide
adjectival drawl to
superlative extremes:

"That man just has
the tee*nine*ciest brain!"

Wee

The small dark hours, yes,
from midnight to dawn—
one, two, three, four, five—
but also a bit
of space, *a short way*

in Scots; awake, though,
it feels so far to
the first hint of light
that means a new day,
nobody alive

but the Lord and me
during the We hours,
that deep thick time ours,
no need for either
to speak or to see.

Dog, Drinking

Not a bowl of tap water

but this muddy puddle
delights our dog, lapping up

rain and runoff, gritty notes

of asphalt and tire rubber
and other eager tongues

that have dipped and slurped

and added their own saliva
to this accidental oasis,

lapping and gulping as if

he hadn't drunk for weeks
and might not drink again,

deep mouth's sloppy happy

long pink muscle unfurling
then curling back, fast,

hard, loud, a splashy pulse

never pausing as he savors
our neighborhood's terroir.

Mutch

*word collected by Horace Kephart
in the North Carolina mountains, 1920s*

Reverse kiss-sound,
smoochy inward noise
we make to call animals,
doubling or tripling
our solo lip-smackings
to persuade them to come
without using the words
they can't speak to us:

maybe we'll be called
in this near-mute way
when we're beyond talk
but still hear everything,
our master mutching us
to rise up and join him
on the other greener side,
to sit, to lie down, to stay.

4.

Smoking

Our professors would bustle into class bearing
the usual stacks of texts and notes and papers

but also a pack of cigarettes in a jacket pocket

which they'd dig out, extracting the hour's first
then lighting up, taking a deep drag, and exhaling,

as most of us did, too, a symposium of smoking,

our breath clouding the room whether we spoke
or not, a smoggy atmosphere for that discussion

of literature written by a fellow chain-smoker,

cheap fuses smoldering in authorial mouth or hand
in the poses affected for publicity photographs:

everybody smoked everywhere, not just my parents

filling dull endless hours of commute and work
and commute and home with dozens of daily fires

set by lighters and extinguished in full ashtrays,

but also fans at games, men after church, teachers
choking their lounge with gossip, movie starlets

blowing oh-oh-oh-oh smoke rings at the ceiling,

and the 1960s governor whose full-length portrait
hanging in the Executive Mansion in Raleigh

shows him with a lit cigarette in his lowered hand,

a product locally grown and locally manufactured,
whose enjoyment imparted a bittersweet soft focus

to everyday details, for smokers and those nearby,

a thin haze nobody really noticed, veiling the view
like background prospects of distant mountains,

their blue gradations disappearing at the horizon.

Portrait of the Poet as Saint Jerome

Master of San Jacopo a Mucciana,
"St. Jerome in His Study", c. 1390

No wonder I look miffed:
all I wanted to do today
was sit here at my desk
in a dazzling crimson robe

inking letters and words
on blank waiting pages,
surrounded by shelves
of books whispering *Write*.

Instead, that miniature lion
is bleeding on the carpet
near my dropped hat,
paw lifted in supplication,

Christ is exsanguinating
on a black cross outside,
His gaunt body ruining
my view of the world,

and the fallen-angel sun
of an ornate gold-leaf halo
makes my big head ache.
Must glory weigh so much?

Lord, all I'd hoped for
on this fine clear morning
was some time to myself
in this study's paradise

to put lines on paper
without such distractions:

no blood, no holy pressure,
just a few precious hours

when, if I'm lucky, my pen
and hand will synchronize,
translating the mysterious
into a common tongue—

what a miracle! I stretch,
then scratch my bad tonsure,
taking three deep breaths
before pronouncing *Amen*.

The Gospel According to Minnie Evans

American outsider artist, 1892-1987

The Eye of God,
her drawings testify,

is plural and symmetrical
and everywhere visible,

it watches our world
from breasts, yes,

and butterflies' hindwings
and visionary plants

unfolding and infolding
their ecstatic colors,

it is not judgmental
but perpetually curious,

a version of Minnie's own
eye and I and aye

centering the blossoming
of her mind and hand

into tendrils and petals
and delicate antennae

in kaleidoscopic patterns
of 3s and 5s and 7s:

this is the good news
of her gardens and dreams,

the gospel her colored pencils
and crayons and oils and inks

kept singing until she finally
ran out of paper and time:

God can only see God
through Creation.

George Washington

the Athenaeum portrait, 1796

He was the unsmiling principal
peering into every American classroom,
his cheeks ruddy and long nose shiny.
Those steady brown eyes missed nothing.

We didn't know that his hair was a wig,
we didn't know that he didn't smile
because he had a new set of false teeth,
we didn't know that we only beheld

one corner of the portrait left unfinished
because Martha didn't much like this likeness,
so why should Gilbert Stuart paint the rest
of George's body below the shoulders,

why not leave most of the primed canvas
a blankness, as if obliterated by fog
rising to erase our country's father
who'd be dead anyway in three years?

Later he became a banknote, legal tender,
blessing the heart of the dollar bill
with a polished version of this same painting
that, cropped, would one day watch me

draw the presidents in my third-grade class,
starting with him, our framed progenitor,
unmoved by my efforts yet strangely flushed,
hoping somebody's hand might get it right.

Autographs

John Lennon, Mickey Mantle, JFK—
my heroes, and I had their autographs

because I'd practiced forging them for years,
studying their variations on X
and mimicking the slant, the loop, the flow
until I could impersonate their names,

a mockingbird of written charisma.

I ruined the sleeves of Beatles 45s
with Liverpudlian aperies from my pen,

I ruined dozens of innocent baseballs
with the rounded cursive of my MM twin,
I ruined sheets of stolen premium bond
with a dead president's cramped John Hancock,

my sister teased me but I didn't care:

autographs were magic, even when scribbled
on a scrap of paper for some cute fan

after a gig, or game, or TV speech,
then imitated later by a boy
who never beheld his heroes in the flesh
but learned to approximate their impish grace,

those ballpoint counterfeits his truest self.

"Richard Burton"

I expected a much more theatrical signature

on the half-title page of *A Christmas Story,*
his slim autobiographical tale about a little boy
and his family in a Welsh mining town,

published in 1964, the same year
he married Elizabeth Taylor the first time

after their affair during shooting *Cleopatra,*

an epic adulterous coupling between stars
so notorious that the Vatican felt compelled
to condemn their "erotic vagrancy."

I thought the hand that lifted all those drinks
and cigarettes to his mellifluous mouth

and pushed black hair away from violet eyes

and gave her a million-dollar diamond
would sign this volume in some reckless way—
a melodramatic spotlight gesticulation.

But he must have been sober on the day
he opened his new book and signed it, the pen

unshaking in his grip as he wrote, neatly:

both cursive names are steady, small, and blue
though the crossbar of the "t" escaped its letter,
headed back east to damp Pontrhydyfen.

"In a Sentimental Mood"

"We had a big dance in a tobacco warehouse,
and afterwards a friend threw a private party
in the North Carolina Mutual building:

everybody was having a bit of sipping

and I was playing piano when another friend
had some trouble with a couple of girls
who were about to start fighting over him,

so I composed this song to calm them down

then and there, on the spot, with a chick
standing beside me on each side of the piano—
one of those spontaneous things, you know,

a single playing—*zhwoop!*—just like that.

After I finished, the gals kissed and made up.
I played it, and I remembered it, and then
I put it down." Monday, April 15, 1935:

nobody breathing can confirm or dispute

the story Duke liked to tell about this song
launched, he said, in Depression-era Durham,
downtown on the upper floors of a building

on Parrish Street, "the Black Wall Street

of America," and recorded in New York City
two weeks later, right after he turned 36.
Ellington is gone, his friends are gone, the women

and their fine dresses and jealousies are gone,

the tobacco warehouse is gone or gone to condos,
the cigarettes and no-longer-Prohibited booze
are gone, the smoke-and-liquor smell is gone,

the piano keys his fingers touched are gone,

the only thing left behind is the song he played,
the one possibly improvised in early spring
ten minutes down the road from where I live,

a melody to lift or divert the heart when things

are going wrong, as things do, while dancing
or flirting or indulging too many bits of sipping,
or when driving around Durham alone, mood

both sentimental and indigo tonight as I listen

to Ellington's sinuous orchestra articulate
the layers of his passionate intelligence
into chords and counterpoints and flourishes

that don't need words to find love's flame

then blow it into a soothing fire and bank it,
those glowing notes helping us to forget
our ache, as Duke may have done that April

when the woman he adored most in this world,

his mother, lay on her deathbed in Detroit,
when he took time on the road, after a long day,

to charm two het-up ladies leaning in on him,

listening, drinking, smoking, admiring the magic
of hands converting trouble to tranquility,
his lucky friend sneaking downstairs and outside,

hiding in dark air sweetened by bright leaf curing.

McAfee's Nonsuch

Apple named for five brothers

who settled in Kentucky after the Revolution
and planted its seeds, which flourished,

the "nonsuch" added to indicate

its excellence as it took root across the region,
a paragon without equal on any tree,

a popular variety also known

as Striped Pearmain, White Crow, Gray's Keeper,
Snorter, Stine, Zeeke, Ladies Favorite—

doomed, over a century ago,

by apple scab or rust, fire blight, mildew, curculio,
poor orchard keepers, changing tastes.

Presumed extinct, it still lives

in this March 1912 watercolor, two views of
a McAfee from Pittston, Pennsylvania,

elevation above, section below:

intact fruit delicately spotted, a sunset yellow
glowing beneath smooth ruddy skin,

halved apple waiting for me

(as it waited for our great-great-great McFees
to slice it up for drying out or bleaching,

for juicy crushing and pressing

into cider sweet or hard, brandy, and vinegar,
for thick apple butter stirred in kettles)

to sniff its wintered-over flesh,

firm, ready to be bitten, the single pip escaped
from its core glistening like a teardrop.